UNIVERSITY
COLLEGE FALMOUTH

— BOOK *of* —

ILLUSTRATED

QUOTES *and* SAYINGS

Paper supplied by Howard Smith Papers

Printed and bound by R Booth Ltd, Mabe, Penryn, Cornwall

Design by Peter Bennett, St Ives

Production Stuart Odgers

Cover Illustration Maria Bovor

ISBN 978-0-9505680-4-1

Becky Guttery

UNIVERSITY
COLLEGE
FALMOUTH

—— BOOK *of* ——

ILLUSTRATED

QUOTES *and* SAYINGS

COMPILED BY THE
BA (HONS) ILLUSTRATION STUDENTS

University College

FALMOUTH

Incorporating **Dartington** College of Arts

BA (hons) Illustration

Joe Skidmore

Emma Metcalfe

This, the third in our series of 'Illustrated Quotes and Sayings' provides art directors and the media industry with further choice regarding the variation and richness of creative talent emerging from Falmouth. Comprising of work by our 2008 graduating students, the book will once again be given a prestigious launch at the Royal Society of Arts in London. The collection of images contained within this book demonstrates our commitment to professionalism, innovation and problem solving combined with the development of a sophisticated and meaningful visual language. We do not discriminate against any style of illustration and the following pages will reveal how diverse and individual our students can be.

Alan Male

Alan Male
Programme Leader
BA (Hons) Illustration

Ella Hudson

Jennifer Crabb

It's my enjoyable task to welcome you to this 2008 Falmouth illustration degree-show book. When I look at it, attractively presented as it is, as usual, I'm irresistibly tempted to compare it to a large box of chocolates, with a wonderful range of assorted centres. There's something for all tastes, some of us will have special favourites, and many, I hope, will be happy to scoff the lot.

After that the comparison doesn't really bear inspection, because once the chocolates are eaten it's all over, whereas here we are actually looking at the beginning of something. Each of these artists has an individual character already, but as they get to work in the world they will be able to respond to a whole range of challenges and develop in all kinds of interesting ways. Strength to their skill and imaginations…..

Sarah Brown

Kayleigh Short

Quentin Blake 2008

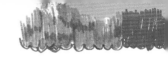

LIV BARGMAN

'Want to be a
film star? Acting
experience not
essential.'

*Roman
Polanski*

'A hug is like a boomerang you get it back right away.' *Bil Keane*

MARIA BOVOR

'The curve is
more powerful
than the sword.'

Mae West

'Logic will get
you from A to B.
Imagination will
take you every-
where.'

Albert Einstein

SARAH BROWN

'Sometimes I've imagined as many as six impossible things before breakfast.'

Lewis Carroll

17

'Jazz is like a
great void, it
waits patiently
until a brave
musician takes
control of space
and time.'

Chris Griffin

KIM-LAM CHAN

'…the stranger drank down the whiskey in one gulp, ate the bucket and spat out the metal components. "Can I get you another?" asked the saloon girl. "Better not," replied the stranger. "Big Jake is coming to town!"'

Alan Male

3

JENNY CORFIELD

'Go out on a
limb.'

Anon

'Every woman should have four pets in her life. A mink in her closet, a jaguar in her garage, a tiger in her bed, and a jackass who pays for everything.'

Paris Hilton

PAULA CRANE

'Of all of our inventions for mass communication, pictures still speak the most universally understood language.'

Walt Disney

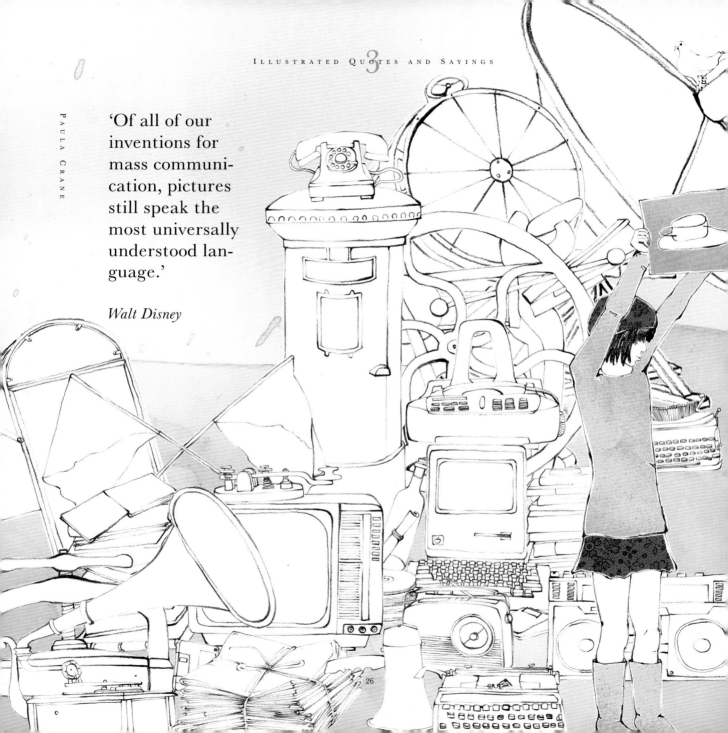

Rosanna Dodd

'I think that in
the future
everyone will be
wearing them.'

Miscellaneous

LAURA ELLIOTT

'If you go down
to the woods
today you're sure
of a big
surprise…'

Jimmy Kennedy
SONGWRITER

'I do not know
how to defeat
others, but
only how to
defeat
myself.'

*Master
Yagyu*

'History, it's just
one bloody thing
after another.'

Herbert Butterfield

SOPHIE FOSTER

34

'She paints her
face to hide her
face.'

Arthur Golden

3

CHARLOTTE GARDINER

'You need chaos
in your soul to
give birth to a
dancing star.'

Nietzsche

'I'm astounded by
people who want
to 'know' the
universe when it's
hard enough to
find your way
around
Chinatown.'

Woody Allen

'Outside of a
dog, a book is a
man's best
friend. Inside of
a dog it's too
dark to read.'

Groucho Marx

WILL GRANT

'Man imitates
nature.'

Seneca

'Please do not feed the seagulls.'

Carrick District Council

'Birds of a feather
flock together.'

Philemon Holland

FLOCK together

CHRIS HARRIS

"MEN ARE NOT PRISONERS OF FATE, BUT ONLY PRISONERS OF THEIR MINDS."

Franklin D. Roosevelt

'In every blossom
there dwelt one
such faery youth
or maiden, but
this one was the
king of all these
flower-spirits.'

*Hans Christian
Andersen*

KATE HINDLEY

'Computers have
a lot of memory,
but not much
imagination.'

Anonymous

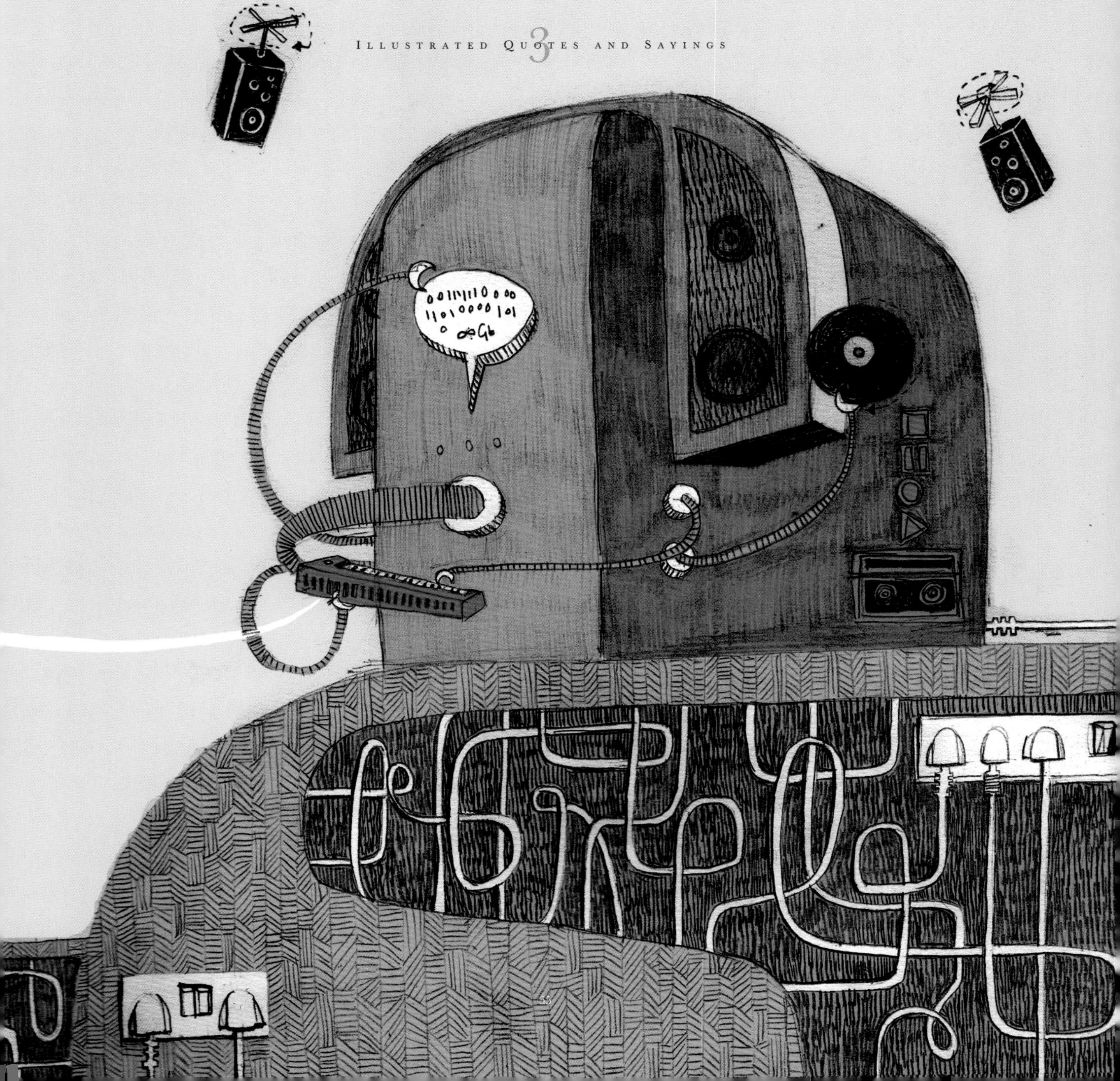
∞Gb

'The essential
joy of being with
horses is that it
brings us in
contact with the
rare elements of
grace, beauty,
spirit and fire.'

Sharon Ralls Lemon

ELLA HUDSON

'I am the lizard king I can do anything!'

Anon

3

AMBERIN HUQ

'Let not light see
my black and
deep desires.'

Macbeth
SHAKESPEARE

'I'd like to be more approach-able not less weird.'

Chloe Sovigny

'The city is built
to music,
therefore never
built at all,
and therefore
built forever.'

Alfred Lord Tennyson

JEREMY JONES

'Peace in Our Time?'

The Independent,
5 May 2012

'I cannot mount
the gibbet like a
saint. It is a
fraud. Nothing's
spoiled by giving
them this lie that
were not rotten
long before.'

*John Proctor
(from 'The Crucible')*

ELINA KALLIO

'If you chase two rabbits both will escape.'

Chinese Proverb

'Minds are like
parachutes – they
only function
when open.'

Thomas Dewar

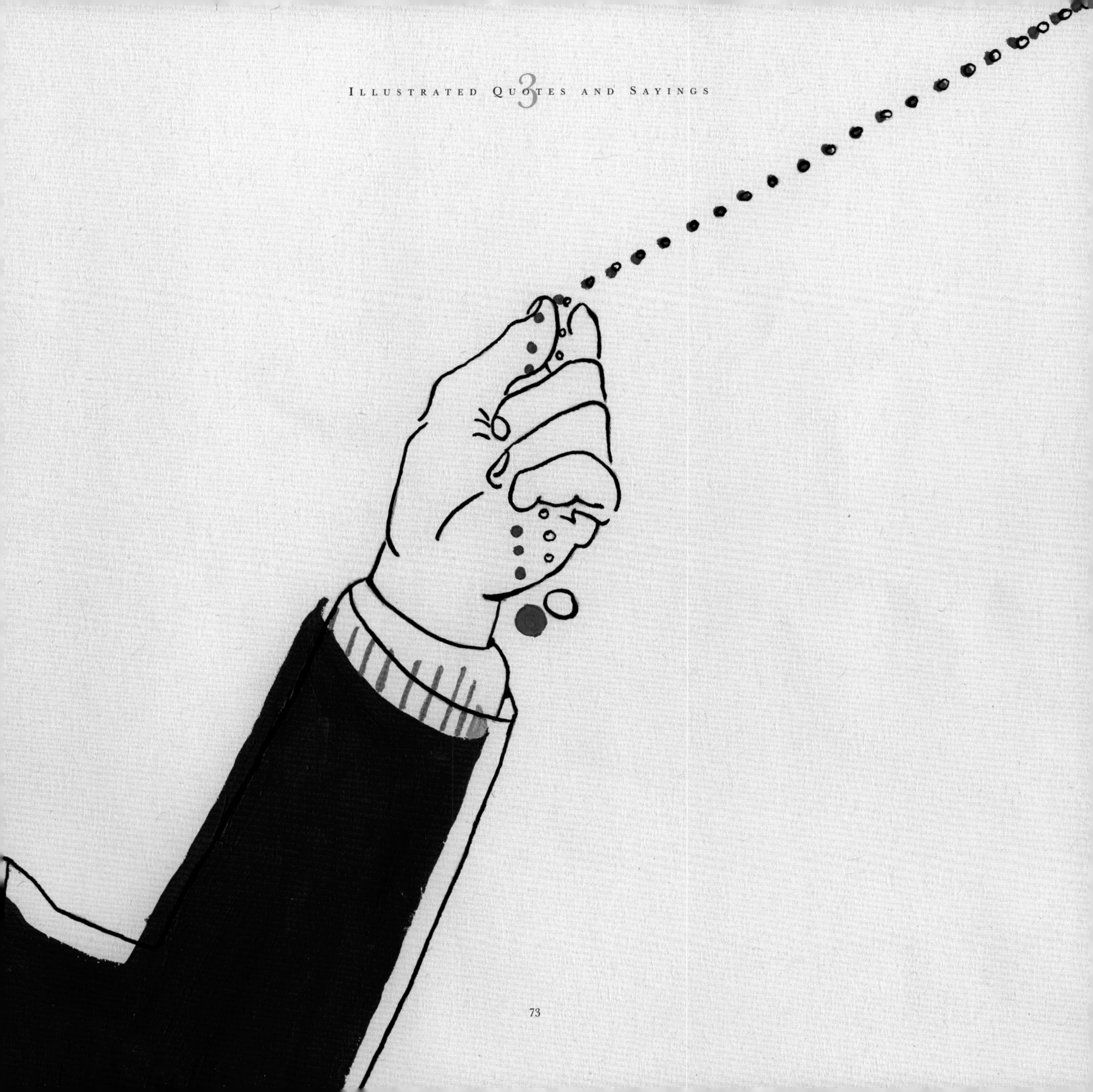

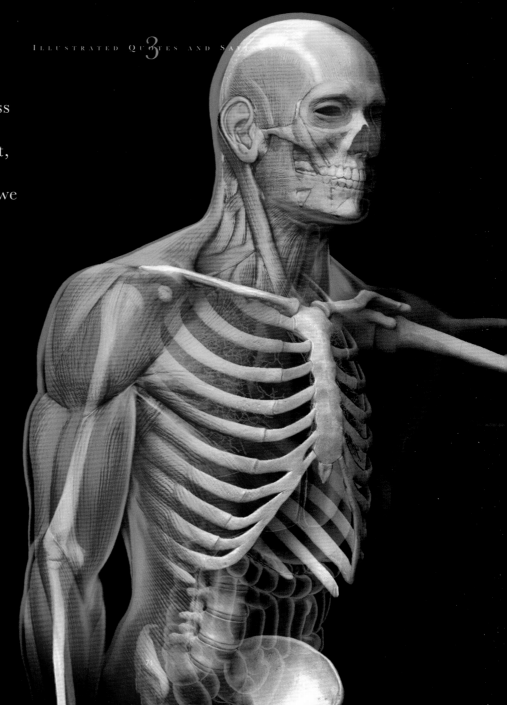

ARRAN LEWIS

'Nothing is less
in our power
than the heart,
and far from
commanding we
are forced to
obey it.'

Jean Jacques
Rousseau

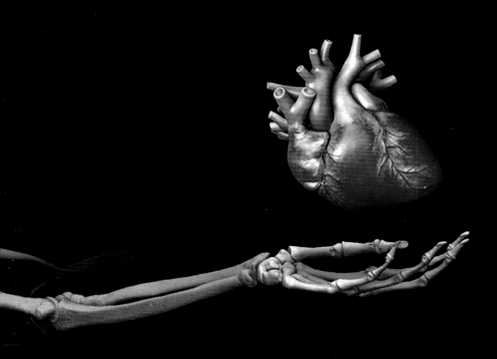

'Ice cream is exquisite. What a pity it isn't illegal.'

Voltaire

MELANIE McPHAIL

'I found out my
sister is my
mum… But
who's my dad?'

From the Jeremy Kyle Show

EMMA METCALFE

A wonderful bird is the pelican,
His bill will hold more than his belican.
He can take in his beak
Food enough for a week,
But I'm damned if I see how the helican.

Dixon Merritt

'Everything you can imagine is real.'

Pablo Picasso

AARON MILLER

82

'I am making no
allegations, just
murder, racism
and cover-ups.'

Mohamed Al Fayed

ALICE NICKLIN

'We are shaped and fashioned by what we love.'

Johann Wolfgang Von Goethe

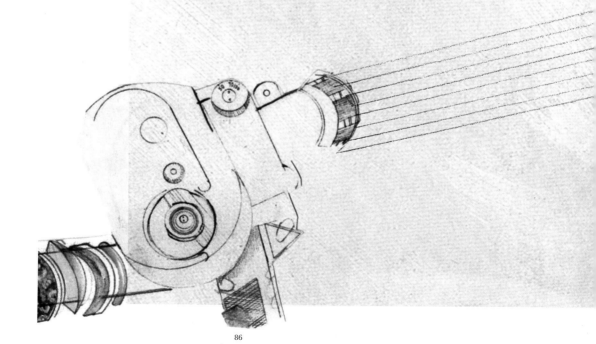

LEE NUTLAND

'In the wild kingdom, you don't live 'till you're ready to die.'

Keith Buckley
EVERY TIME I DIE

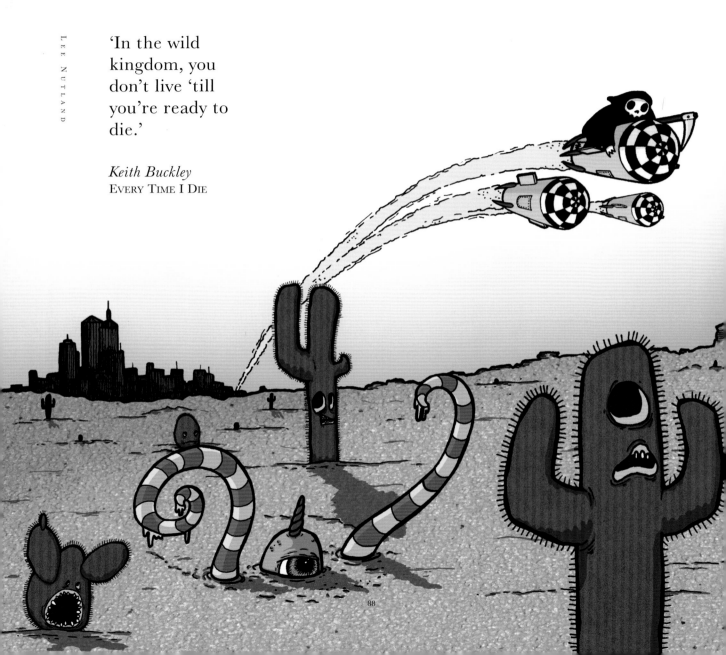

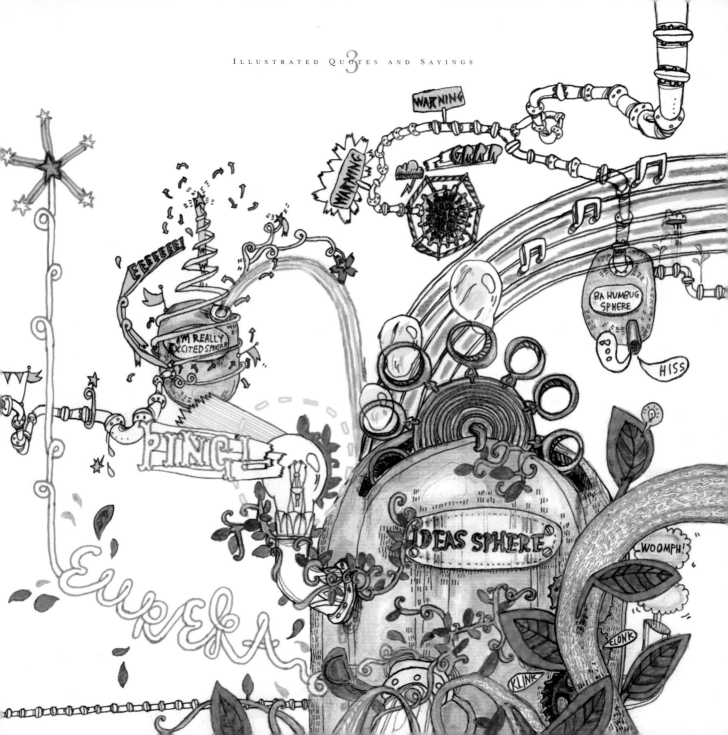

'I have studied many philoso- phers and many cats. The wisdom of cats is infinitely superior.'

Hippolyte Taine

3

'For the fairest one.'

Judgement of Paris,
GREEK MYTHOLOGY

RACHAEL RYDER

'Flying without
feathers is not
easy.'

Titus Maccius Plautus

KAYLEIGH SHORT

'The early bird
may get the
worm, but the
second mouse
gets the cheese.'

Anonymous

LIZ SNOOK

'Too many cooks
spoil the broth.'

Proverb

ROMEO IS BLEEDING

HE GAVE THE MAN HIS TICKET
AND CLIMBED A BALCONY AT THE
MOVIES

AND HE DIED
WITHOUT A WHIMPER
LIKE EVERY HERO'S DREAM
LIKE AN ANGEL WITH A BULLET
AND CAGNEY ON THE SCREEN.

→ TOM WAITS

CLAUDIA STARBUCK

'I wanna go
where there ain't
no snow…'

Burl Ives,
THE BIG ROCK CANDY
MOUNTAIN

'The table is rumbling,
The glass is moving,
No, I was not pushing
that time,
It spells…P.U.S.H.O
double F.'

Morrissey

ALEXIA TUCKER

'A tree is a living
thing, not that
different from a
tall, leafy dog
that has roots
and is very quiet.'

Jack Handy
ENVIRONMENTALIST

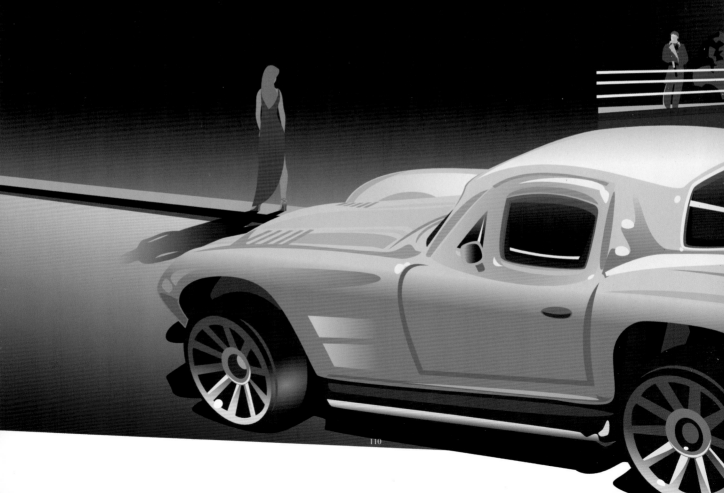

'A city is more
than a place in
space, it is a
drama in time.'

Sir Patrick Geddes

PATRICK WELHAM

'Think outside
the box.'

Anon

UNIVERSITY
COLLEGE FALMOUTH
— BOOK of —
ILLUSTRATED
3
CONTACTS

B

Liv Bargman
The Armoury
Kerry Street
Montgomery
Powys, Montgomeryshire
SY15 6RJ

M: 07854339697
E: oliviabargman@hotmail.co.uk
W: livbargman.co.uk

Hetty Blair
Backwell Hill Cottage
Backwell Hill
Backwell
BS48 3DA

M: 07824817952
E: hairyhetty@hotmail.com
W: hettyblair.co.uk

Maria Bovor
68 Rynal Place
Evesham
Worcestershire
WR11 4PZ

M: 07929456575
E: Apricotmuffins@hotmail.com
W: mariabovor.co.uk

Lucy Brockman
8 Holker Road
Buxton
Derbyshire
SK17 6QN

M: 07875564896
E: lucybrockman@hotmail.com
W: www.lucybrockman.co.uk

Sarah Brown

M: 07841647545
E: sarahbrownillustration@yahoo.com
W: sarahbrownillustration.co.uk

C

Kin-lam Chan

T: +852 27501026 Hong Kong
M: +44 (0)7799876675
     +44 (0)7828322785
E: kennethchankinlam@yahoo.com.hk
W: kinlamchan.co.uk

Katie Collins
Brackenbury
Westcliff, Porthtowan
Truro
Cornwall
TR4 8AE

M: 07969292890
E: katiecollins86@hotmail.com
W: katiecollinsillustration.co.uk

Jenny Corfield
27 Franks Avenue
Hereford
HR2 6HZ

M: 07792325487
E: jennycorfield@hotmail.com
W: jennycorfield.co.uk

Jennifer Crabb
Midaway Yeovilton
Ilchester
Somerset
BA22 8EZ

M: 07790085564
E: jennifercrabb@hotmail.com
W: jennifercrabb.co.uk

Erlend Espedal
Flyplassveien 6
3728 Skien
Norway

M: 07833942784
E: staalpete@yahoo.com
W: erlendespedalillustration.com

Paula Crane
10 Bentswood Cresent
Haywards Heath
West Sussex
RH16 3QR

M: 07773118897
E: crane.paula@googlemail.com
W: paulacrane.co.uk

 F

Sophie Foster
Little Brook
Huish Episcopi
Langport
Somerset
TA10 9QT

M: 07763357502
E: sophie.foster@yahoo.co.uk
W: sophiefoster.co.uk

D

Rosanna Dodd
Rosebank
Silver Street
Congresbury
North Somerset
BS49 5EY

M: 07950585989
E: rosad@hotmail.co.uk
W: rosadodd.co.uk

Abi French
33, Bronsecombe Close
Penryn
Cornwall
UK
TR10 8LE

M: 07786531171
E: abi.french@hotmail.co.uk
W: abiillustration.co.uk

E

Laura Elliott
8 Helston Road
Nailsea
North Somerset
BS48 2UA

M: 07840450470
E: laurae2003@hotmail.com
W: lauraelliottillustration.co.uk

G

Charlotte Gardiner

M: 07791524865
E: charlotte_gardiner@hotmail.co.uk
W: charliesillustrations.co.uk

Cally Gibson
23 Braemar Avenue
London
N22 7BY

M: 07909530434
E: callygibsonillustration@hotmail.co.uk
W: www.callygibson.co.uk

Becky Guttery
Bonnington
Vicarage Road, South Clifton
Notts
NG23 7AQ

M: 07986156534
E: greekgirlfriend@live.co.uk
W: greekgirlfriend.com

Jonny Glover
23 Kerrison Road, Ealing
London W5 5NW

M: 07807425196
E: jonnyglover@googlemail.com
W: www.jonnyglover.co.uk

Chris Harris
90 Pemberton Park
Llanelli
Camarthanshire
SA14 8RW

M: 07886035117
E: chrisharrisillustration@gmail.com
W: chrisharrisillustration.com

Will Grant
21 Tollgate Road
Salisbury
Wiltshire
SP1 2JA

M: 07886627977
E: willgrantillustration@hotmail.co.uk
W: willgrantillustration.co.uk

Sally Haysom

M: 07737779870
E: sallyhaysom@hotmail.com
W: sallyhaysomillustration.co.uk

Richard Green
Flat 4
7 Woodlane Crescent
Falmouth
Cornwall, TR11 4QS

M: 07731865818
E: richardgreen349@live.co.uk
W: richardgreenillustration.co.uk

Kate Hindley
20 Parkstone Avenue
Hill Top
Bromsgrove
Worcestershire
B61 7NS

T: 07913019530
E: hindley.kate@googlemail.com
W: katehindley.co.uk

Autumn Hoyle
Tyddyn Ucha Farm
Llangernyw
Nr Abergele, Conwy
North Wales, LL22 8PS

T: 01745860376
M: 07789158973
E: autumn_hoyle@hotmail.co.uk
W: autumnhoyle.co.uk

Anna Jones
Rhiwfa
Beach Road
Penmaenmawr
Conwy
N.Wales, LL326AY

M: 07876213237
E: arpink@hotmail.co.uk
W: roborainbow.com

Ella Hudson
6 Albert Terrace
Penzance
Cornwall
TR18 2DD

T: 01736 366313
M: 07773332494
W: ellahudsonillustration.co.uk

Jeremy Jones

M: 07802619016
E: jeremyjones@live.co.uk
W: jezjonesillustration.com

Amberin Huq
57 West Drive
South Cheam
Surrey
SM2 7NB

M: 07849943133
E: amberin.h@hotmail.com
W: amberinhuq.co.uk

Martin Jump
40 Cremyll Road
Torpoint
Cornwall
PL11 2DY

M: 07828940826
E: martin.jump@virgin.net
W: martinjumpillustration.co.uk

Ruth-Ann Ivory
34 Croyland Drive
Elstow
Bedfordshire
MK42 9GH

M: 07966386110
E: ruthannivory7@hotmail.com
W: ruthannivory.co.uk

Elina Kallio

M: 07870103029
E: elina.illustration@gmail.com
W: www.elinakallio.co.uk

Hannah Kennard
Southview
The Lane, Randwick
Stroud
Gloucestershire
GL6 6HN

M: 07812772449
E: hannahkennard@hotmail.com
W: hannahkennard.co.uk

72

Emma Metcalfe

M: 07743420084
E: info@emillustration.co.uk
W: emillustration.co.uk

80

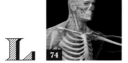

Arran Lewis

M: 07917692721
E: info@arranlewis.co.uk
W: arranlewis.co.uk

74

Aaron Miller
62 Naunton Lane
Leckhampton
Cheltenham
Gloucestershire
Gl53 7BH

M: 07732884815
E: aaron@aaronmillerillustration.com
W: aaronmillerillustration.com

82

Molly Maine
217 Clive Road
London
SE21 8DG

M: 07904963591
E: molly.maine@yahoo.com
W: mollymaine.com

76

Bob Moran
Holly Cottage
Bewley Down
Axminster
Devon
EX13 7JX

M: 07892790024
E: bobmoran@hotmail.co.uk
W: bobmoran.co.uk

84

Melanie McPhail
46 Captain Fold Road
Little Hulton
Worsley
Manchester
M38 9SX

M: 07926849338
E: melly_mcphail@hotmail.co.uk
W: melanie-mcphail.com

78

Alice Nicklin
Littlecote
The Warren
Mayfield
East Sussex
TN20 6UB

M: 07765465116
E: Alicenicklinillustration@yahoo.com
W: alicenicklin.co.uk

86

Lee Nutland
92 Glenthorne Avenue
Yeovil
Somerset
BA21 4PW

M: 07780608760
E: lee_nutland@hotmail.co.uk
W: leenutland.com

Kayleigh Short
88 Cherry Garden Road
Eastbourne
East Sussex
BN20 8HF

M: 07940326339
E: rats1985@hotmail.com
W: kayleighshort.co.uk

Hannah Postlethwaite
9 Moor Row
Ireleth
Askam-in-Furness
Cumbria
LA16 7EX

M: 07732745803
E: hannahpos@yahoo.co.uk
W: hannahposillustration.co.uk

Joe Skidmore

M: 07837812168
E: joe_skid@hotmail.co.uk
W: www.joeskid.co.uk

Harriet Rowe

M: 07792628783
E: harrietrowe@gmail.com
W: harrietrowe.co.uk

Liz Snook
15 Central Avenue
Pinner
Middlesex
HA5 5BT

E: lizthesnookcocker@hotmail.com
W: lizsnook.co.uk

Rachael Ryder
12 Townstal Cres
Dartmouth, Devon
TQ6 9JH

M: 07789956383
E: rachaelryder@hotmail.co.uk
W: rachaelryderillustration.co.uk

Benjamin Southan
69 Priory Road
Hastings
East Sussex
TN34 3JJ

M: 07890607280
E: ben.southan@virgin.net
W: benjaminsouthan.co.uk

Claudia Starbuck

M: 07941980650
E: claudiastarbuck@hotmail.com
W: claudiastarbuck.com

Alexia Tucker

M: 07875166672
E: alexiatucker@hotmail.com
W: alexiatuckerillustration.com

T

Tamsyn Swingler
28 Upton Towans
'Calador'
Hayle, Cornwall
TR27 5BJ

T: 01736 753057
M: 07944336616
E: tamsynswingler@gmail.com
W: tamsynswingler.co.uk

Patrick Welham
12 Jamaica Terrace
Heamoor
Penzance, Cornwall
TR18 3HQ

T: 01736 361720
M: 07811989665
E: patrickwelham@hotmail.com
W: patrick-welham.co.uk

W

Laurie Woodruff

M: 07913767104
E: lauriew@hotmail.co.uk
W: lauriewoodruff.com

University
College Falmouth
BA (hons) Illustration
Staff

Alan Male	Course Leader & Level Three Tutor
Mark Foreman	Level Two Tutor
Nigel Owen	Level One Tutor
Sue Clarke	Senior Lecturer
Keryn Roach	Senior Lecturer
Mike Venning	Senior Lecturer
Serena Rodgers	Senior Lecturer
Linda Scott	Illustration

Gary Long	Life drawing
Rachel Dunn	Visual studies
Mary Mabbutt	Visual studies
Sue Miller	Art direction
Peter Bennett	Graphic design
Stuart Odgers	Printing technology
Karenanne Knight	Creative writing

Liv Bargman

Rosanna Dodd

Jonny Glover

Arran Lewis

Charlotte Gardiner

Sally Haysom

Aaron Miller

Chris Harris

Ruth-Ann Ivory

Hannah Postlethwaite

Will Grant

Tamsyn Swingler

Bob Moran

Lee Nutland

Rachael Ryder

—Book of—

Quotes *and* Sayings

3